IF I KNEW THEN, WHAT I KNOW NOW: Wisdom for Young Psychiatrists, Psychologists, Counselors, and Other Helping Professionals.

Peter A. Olsson MD

INTRODUCTION

Thirteen postgraduate years studying and working to be a psychiatrist and psychoanalyst, but not one lecture or seminar about the practicalities of practicing psychiatry, psychoanalysis or psychotherapy? No supervisory dialogue with teacher psychiatrists in private practice covered any of the key psychological pitfalls?   In the early 1970s when this dinosaur trained it seemed to be assumed that the private office practice of psychiatry or psychotherapy was the preferred goal for which all we resident physicians, the psychology fellows, and psychiatric social work trainees should aspire. During residency training none of my supervisors opined about what kind of psychiatry I seemed to be best suited for. In-patient psychiatry? Psychotherapy (Psychoanalysis/Group/Family/Individual psychotherapy ?) , Forensic? Research? (Basic/Clinical), Psychiatric teaching? Administration? General Psychiatry? Public Sector/VA/Community Mental Health? Emergency psychiatry?

 I now think that toward the end of my training years I should have asked for my respected teachers and supervisors' opinions about this topic. It is like my mother once said, "If you had asked me about whether a girl you were dating would make a good wife for you and you a husband for her, I would have been glad to give my opinion, but you never asked…."

Perhaps faculties of psychiatric training programs , clinical psychology programs, and psychiatric social work training programs should develop formal and structured ways to deliver peer and faculty feedback about this subspecialty issue to trainees soon to graduate. One domain of this feedback in strict confidence should include, "It is best that you don't enter psychiatry or psychotherapy practice" with reasons given and another area of medicine, psychology or social work recommended to the colleague.

Also un-addressed during my training were the important practical, financial, ethical, and personal issues to be considered by any psychiatrist or therapist in the day-to-day 'Real World' after training? Like most psychiatric residents, I had excellent lectures, journal clubs, seminars and supervisors. But, other than observing supervisors' practices, and making inferences about those observations, I had no organized teaching experience or orientation about the "Real World" of professional life as a psychiatrist. Few supervisors shared what impact practicing psychiatry or psychoanalysis had on their marriage, family, social and inner life.

My young colleagues giving feedback about this book also had the integrity and strength to suggest that much of my book was cathartic of my personal and partially unresolved painful experiences and agendas from my training and 30+ years of practice. They were right on target! I even considered writing two books. The second book would be called, "Reminiscences, Lamentations and Remonstrance's of a Psychiatric/Psychoanalytic Dinosaur", or "Grumblings of a Grumpy Old Psychiatrist".

Chapter I---THINGS I WISH A PSYCHIATRIST 'MOTHER HEN' or 'DUTCH UNCLE' HAD TAUGHT ME.

MARRIAGE

No marriage relationship is easy to work out over time. Some psychiatrists and therapists I am acquainted with think that the biological and evolutionary imperatives in the human animal are not compatible with monogamy or marriage. I agree with the observation that evolutionary and biological perspectives are valuable in psychotherapeutic understanding of patients (i.e. Glantz & Pearce*). But, I disagree with the idea that human nature is incompatible with monogamy and a happy or contented marriage. One of the higher levels of the evolution of human consciousness and accomplishment is the transcendence of our elemental narcissism and biologically based aggression and lust. With mindfulness of our life partner's needs, a good sense of humor, and integrity---contentment and joy are possible in our marriages. It does take effort however, and plenty of patience and creativity. If your marriage is not working, seek marital consultation and or therapy. If your spouse refuses to participate, seek a divorce lawyer and don't smolder in your unhappiness. Inform your spouse of your feelings and plans during every step of this process. My difficult advice on this matter----don't get involved in a new relationship until the divorce is final. If you have the strength of character to be able to do this, you will be far more likely to be happy or content in your next marriage.

One key issue is **TIME**. If you are single, time with significant others is still important, and hopefully you will find a **Life Partner**. People with life partners live longer and have better physical and mental health. Our work as psychiatrists is very time bound and time determined. The thirty or forty five-minute hour rules most of our day. We get paid by the hour if we work in a private practice. Even if we work for a salary at a community mental health center, a VA hospital or other institution, the time demands are also present. Our work is emotionally draining. When we get home at five or six PM, (Usually it gets later), we are emotionally drained. Our spouse is also tired from homemaking or their work outside the home. I believe that taking care of several children for an eight to nine hour day is much more draining than any psychiatrists work day!

A vigorous thirty-minute walk together before or after supper is ideal. Jogging, swimming, or bicycling is less effective for associated couple communication during the activity. Gardening together, while less aerobically beneficial, can allow for communication and winding down emotionally. Ripping out a weed can sublimate those pent-up hostilities. It is certainly worth paying a baby sitter for this time together.

In 1985, Daniel Goleman** reviewed the research literature on Marital Happiness and contentment. Contentment correlated strongly with whether a couple had twenty to thirty minutes to talk meaningfully together daily. He found that couples developed a unique language or emotional shorthand that evolved in a special way in their relationship. There was no correlation with IQ, presence of psychopathology, or level of sexual satisfaction.

In 1988, O'Leary and Malone*** followed 292 white, suburban, middle class couples from New York from six weeks before marriage until three years into their marriage. Their findings were similar to Goldman's earlier findings. O'Leary and Malone's interviews and questionnaires revealed predictors of marital success or distress. They found that after 2.5 years 25% of the marriages were in distress. Key triggers for distress were aggressive verbal fights about money, sex and in-laws. Key positive factors were good daily communication and verbal / nonverbal signs of affection, (holding hands, kissing and being greeted warmly).

A corollary to O'Leary and Malone's findings that I have noticed is that it is good to share friends you make at work with your spouse. If you begin to share more about your life with a coworker than you do with your spouse, it can lead naturally to falling in love with that person. If the coworker and or their spouse were good people, you would want them to share time with you and your life-partner as couples.

Patients in psychotherapy or psychotherapeutically informed psychopharmacology form a **Special Pedestal** of **Idealization** for us. It is often very pleasant, flattering and affirming to our narcissism. But, it should not be taken too seriously. Our patients put us on a pedestal to try to compensate for the neglect, weakness, or physical /emotional abuse they perceived in relationship with their parents, siblings, grandparents or other adults. Our spouse or life partner often feels like they cannot compete with the special intimacy time our patients receive from us every day. It takes conscious effort to counteract this "Spell of 'wonderfulness'" that we can allow our patients to provide for us, sometimes to the subtle exclusion of our spouse.

The other extreme from the special pedestal is the **Pit** of **Devaluation,** when patients enact the rage, disappointment and sadness 'as if' we were the bad parent or other figure from their past pain and sorrow. It takes conscious effort to not take this devaluation experience home with us. Don't withdraw from your family as if to protect them from this stored-up stuff left over from the office or hospital. Or, don't be like the person who is blistered with hostile criticism by their boss, only to come home to yell at the family and kick the family dog.

The Impact of Psychiatric and Psychotherapeutic WORK on Our Inner Self

There are two ends of an emotional spectrum that characterize the way we psychiatrists protect ourselves from the painful things we hear about at work. At one extreme is a cool, aloof, detached, pseudoscientific, 'objective' or cynical attitude. The other extreme is over-identification with our patients leading to soul-sadness, potential burnout, or existential depression. A supportive, happy, or contented marriage takes effort, but when combined with a well-rounded life, helps to prevent divorce, burnout or both. I recommend frequent reading of Kahill Gibran's mystical poem about marriage***** from his book, *The Prophet* (1923, pp15-16). In regard to our marriages and life- partners, ponder what Homer said hundreds of years B.C. in, THE ODESSY, Book VI, lines180-185:

> "And may the gods accomplish your desire:
> a home, a husband, and harmonious
> converse with him--the best thing in the world
> being a strong house held in serenity
> where man and wife agree. Woe to their enemies,
> joy to their friends! But all this they know best."

YOUR CHILDREN

The famous psychoanalyst Heinz Kohut whose ideas founded Self Psychology (1977****), treated many adult children of psychiatrists, psychoanalysts, psychologists and psychiatric social workers. Kohut found that these persons had had unsuccessful previous psychotherapies because of a common pattern of experience they had with their psychotherapist parents. Kohut observed that these people had a vague sense of not being real. This was particularly true about their inability to experience emotions. Kohut also found that they had an intense but conflicted need to attach themselves to powerful people in their environment in order to feel alive. Kohut discovered that their parents frequently and in detail, communicated their empathic insights about what they (the children) thought, wished and felt. These parents were not hostile, cold or rejecting. But, their seeming to know more about the child than the child himself knew about himself, created interference with the full consolidation of their selves. I have in my own practice, observed this same pattern in children of psychiatrists. One young adult patient of mine whose father was a psychiatrist-psychoanalyst said:

> "Around my dad I feel transparent, 'seen through', like he reads my mind and feelings."

Kohut advocated treating these persons detachment not as a 'resistance' to be confronted, but as a haven they needed earlier in life to avoid being penetrated by their parent's misguided empathy. In the present therapy they could learn to effectively identify their own feelings for themselves. They no longer needed any guru. They could be their own genuine self. After several years of work in therapy my patient who was the noted psychiatrist-analyst's son told me about a New Yorker cartoon that had become his favorite. In the cartoon, a psychiatrist is hitting his patient on the couch over the head with his shoe--- exclaiming: "It might have been right, even if your father said so!"

So, I struggled hard to not act as interpreting 'shrink' to my own children! My natural tendency in parenting was always to be over-protective, so I have always found the existential meaning behind Kahlil Gibran's poem about children, *The Prophet* (1923, pp17-18)***** to be helpful in my parenting efforts.

I thought of this poem countless times during my struggles and efforts to be a parent to my three children.

The TIME thing also affects our children. I made great efforts to spend as much time as possible with my children. I found that doing ordinary tasks together, like racking leaves, taking walks, pulling weeds or watching TV together was best. Elaborate, expensive vacations to interesting places are nice but pillow fights and floor wrestling are OK too. Reading stories to kids or making them up at bedtime or at campfires is good. When TV shows hit heavy topics it is important to talk about violence, death, love, etc I tried to let them see my playful side. This was not easy for a serious intellectual like me. Smile. I tried to let them see my mistakes. The dignified acknowledgement of a mistake or offering an apology is as valuable for our kids to witness as our financial or professional triumphs. Do enjoyable things with your children. Let them have choices and be prepared to listen and talk at times when you are least ready for it. Like driving home late from an event when you are hungry or tired. There is something inherently beneficial about conversations with kids that occur while driving, hiking or walking. Kids don't feel stared-at or under pressure because both persons have to watch where they are going as they talk.

I was once treating the wife of a child psychiatrist. He worked nine or ten hours per day and Saturday mornings till noon. His wife described an amazing event. Their ten-year-old son knew that his dad worked without a secretary on Saturday mornings. The resourceful lad rode his bike the six blocks to his dad's office at 10:30 on a Saturday morning. He put his own name in the schedule book for the last therapy appointment at 11 AM. When the doctor came out after his last patient, there was his own son. This event got a message through to our colleague that his wife and I had not been able to get across at many joint therapy sessions.

COMMUNITY

Service to your community on a pro bono basis is very important. It is further down the priority list than you health, your marriage and your family, but it entwines with the other priorities. Talks, lectures, church and community activities and service do help with drumming up referrals and consultations for a private practice. But, community service serves other purposes. It brings you in contact with caring and most likely more normal folks than you see during your workday. I can recall participating in a schoolyard cleanup with my wife and children. Our children made new friends and so did my wife and I. I can't stress enough the need for therapists to associate with "NORMAL" caring, friendly and ordinary people. Some of our patients are fairly normal but our relationship with them focuses around problem areas and frankly, many of our patients are quite troubled persons and we need time away from them.

AVOCATION/HOBBIES

I was able to start avocational interests and hobbies early. (Poetry & Prose writing and sketching). In one sense this early development of a hobby or carving out time in my schedule for one I already had, was a form of early retirement planning. There is also some solid evidence that staying intellectually active prevents or postpones Alzheimer's.

The time spent in making pottery, painting, music, poetry/ prose writing, music, woodwork, etc provides time to be by yourself. These quiet investments in creative activity provide some respite from the pressures and tension of psychiatric work. They are also elegant forms of "burnout" prevention.

I once co-led a weekend "burn-out" prevention workshop for a group of psychiatrists. We used clay, paints, woodcarving materials, writing pads, books of poetry and some musical instruments. Each session started with a very brief talk/discussion on "Burn-out", some music and mindfulness meditation, and then 'Free Time'. One psychiatrist did not say a word the entire weekend. He listened but he mainly sculpted quietly in clay. As the weekend went on his sculpture emerged in the form of a graceful bird in flight. At the very last hour of wrap-up he said: "I have not felt so relaxed or content in a long time. I wish I had started this sculpting activity on a regularly scheduled basis twenty years ago!"

During my training in psychiatry we may have talked about patients who were vocationally burned out. But, it seemed to be assumed that our profession is so fascinating and wonderful that we would never get burned out or consider a career direction change. That was nonsense!

Chapter II---THE UNMENTIONABLE TOPIC: PSYCHIATRIST/PSYCHOTHERAPIST BURNOUT.

Definitions:

Burnout is the psychological state of being exhausted, bored or disillusioned with one's profession, job or major life activity.

Psychiatrist Impairment is physical or emotional illness that is directly connected with ineffective, incompetent or unethical performance as a psychiatrist. A burned out psychiatrist is often impaired but not always. A burned out psychiatrist may do adequate or barely competent work. Even above average work can be done by a previously superior psychiatrist who is burned out.

Mental Illness of a psychiatrist is the presence in him or her of psychosis, neurosis, organic brain disease, addiction, drug misuse or character disorder. These conditions usually but not always cause impairment of work function.

Many but not all psychiatrists should change career directions or change careers entirely at least once. If you keep pushing yourself to go to your hospital or office and dreaming of other fast fading destinies---stop and think.

Symptoms of Burnout

The symptoms of burnout are remarkably similar to depression but slightly less intense and morevague. Chronic fatigue with no medical explanation is quite a common symptom of burnout. It is not repaired by sleep or napping, and only briefly alleviated or sometimes worsened by a vacation. Attitudes associated with burnout are; nagging boredom; humorless cynicism; greedy obsessions about money; lessened enthusiasm about one's own marriage or family; distorted time perception, (never enough time or time seeming endless); and most serious of all, decreased depth of friendships. In the advanced stage of burnout there is apathy, emotional detachment and meaningless sexual affairs. Often a burned out psychiatrist's sexual affairs and boundary crossings are with patients or ex-patients.

Special Difficulties and Situations Involved with Psychiatrist/Psychotherapist Burnout

The job of a psychiatrist/psychotherapist is never done. New evaluations of people in significant emotional pain await us at the office or hospital every day. Former patients that had a successful result, return with a recurrence. A psychiatrist-therapist cannot easily tell if his or her work is having results. An architect, contractor or house painter can see tangible results. We psychiatrists rarely hear from a happy and satisfied customer. Psychiatrists see so many diverse people with complicated problems. Only politicians deal with such intense an array of expectations. Many of our patients present with an endlessly draining neediness that can lead to our feeling sucked dry. As a VA resident on call I had a dream that there was a drive up window outside the day hospital with a gigantic red white and blue breast protruding for endless use by patients. We psychiatrists work in a setting of great emotional intensity that demands high degrees of affective awareness; control of our emotions; accurate empathy; and tolerance of ambiguity, uncertainty and occasionally danger. We are often required to provide an empathic mirror for our patients but we also can see upsetting things in ourselves mirrored back to us from our patients. When we hear exciting, fascinating, terrible or astounding things from our patients we must not tell them to friends or ever gossip about them. The seeming quiet and sedentary world of a psychiatrist or psychotherapist's office can be emotionally draining and soul-saddening beyond belief.

I want to share a poem written about the charged atmosphere of psychotherapy written by a psychiatrist at a burn out workshop where expressive arts techniques were used.

DEAFENING ECHOES OF PAIN
[Psychiatrist's inner thoughts]

Transcendent trust, fragile, in a fabric of woven projections.
[Damn it, I'm not your mother!]

Allowing your pain to become almost mine again and again.
[When will this therapy hour be up?!]

Fears and tears from facing sad claims of years past.
[Not that angry look again as you leave.]

How many glances inward and backward do you dare?
[Now you are acting like MY father!]

All those twists and turns of your guts and mine.
[God! I'm hungry for a snack.]

Another chartered neurosis map, of your shared pain.
[I want to scream , or smoke a cigarette!]

Hate me again as proxy for cruel memories avoided.
[Damn your parents anyway!]

Attack me in this strange love-hate transference game.
[Where is my supervisor now?]

Whining about uncertainty compounded and confounded.
[Fire me! I'll give your money back.]

Finally through insight comes mastery of yesterdays .
[Don't leave me now]

The goodbye beacon of your insights freedom
[Don't go, I just started to like you!]

Forget me, by knowing you
[Not another new evaluation next hour!]

Prevention and Cure for Psychiatrist/Psychotherapist Burnout

My earlier observations about regular exercise and quality time with your spouse and

children are important for burnout prevention. I also suggest that you find some artistic activity that

is your special private activity. Some psychiatrists I have known are artists in their work. But, I am

talking about music, crafts, painting, sculpting, sketching, gardening, carpentry, etc. Spend regular

time developing this for yourself now, and don't wait until that future mythical time when you

"Retire".

Friendship is one of the sure preventions of burnout. A colleague who is a true and deeply

valued friend is a treasure, but make as many quality friends as you can. In the only paper in the

psychoanalytic literature "ON FRIENDSHIP" (1963, J. of The American Psychoanalytic

Association) Leo Rangel offers this definition of friendship, (p11). "Friendship is a deep, kind, enduring affection, founded on mutual respect and esteem." The work, play and joy you build in your life by being a good friend is better than compounded interest in the best mutual fund you can find. The loneliness, stress and emotional depletion that psychiatric practice brings, requires special joys like a good friend away from the world of patients. Gibran's poem about friendship from *The Prophet* (1923, pp 58-59)***** is worth reading many times..

Sometimes a career-shift or change in direction is the only cure for burnout. Twenty years into my practice of psychoanalysis, general psychiatry and psychotherapy a good friend and colleague challenged me with the following:

"Peter, when are you going to quit treating those wealthy worried well, and treat the really mentally ill?"

I gave it a lot of thought, and when my wife found a job she liked many states away, I took a job at a community mental health center working with a team that treated chronically and severely mentally ill patients. That career change helped me to feel rejuvenated and challenged for the last decade of my practice of psychiatry. Don't be afraid of a career-shift if it fits you.

My mother/father hen pontifications may amuse you, annoy you, or interest you, but they are offered sincerely. I hope you will heed many of them early in your practice. They get more difficult to adopt as the years of your practice fly by.

References Chapter II

*   Glantz,K. and Pearce, J. (1989) EXILES FROM EDEN: Psychotherapy From an Evolutionary Perspective. W. W. Norton& Company, New York and London.

**   Goleman,D. "Marriage: Research Reveals Ingredients of Happiness." The New York Times, Section C, April 16, 1985.

***O'Leary and Malone, J summarized in "Building a Happy Marriage" by Schoonmaker,M.E. THE HOUSTON POST, Tuesday, October 18, 1988, Section B, pp1-2.

****Kohut,H. (1977), THE RESTORATION OF THE SELF. International Universities Press, Inc. New York, pp146-151.

*****Gibran, K.(1923) Marriage, pp 15-16)"Speak to Us of Children" (1923 pp 17-18) and Friendship (1823 pp.58-59). In THE PROPHET. Alfred A. Knopf (1979) New York,

Chapter III---ON MENTORING, MOTIVATION, AND MONEY AS MOTIVATION IN A PSYCHIATRIC/PSYCHOTHERAPY CAREER

As my years in practice proceeded rapidly, I have found that mentoring and being mentored is not just 'Icing on the cake', but it can be a large piece of 'the cake' of professional and personal life. We are most fortunate as psychiatrists if we have had good (not perfect) mentors. Any good mentor, like a caring parent, hopes that his student will eventually no longer need him or her. Good mentors and teachers hope that the student will carry the personal and professional torch further than they did in achievements and satisfactions.

NEUROSIS AS MOTIVATION OR IMPEDIMENT IN BEING A PSYCHIATRIST

How Mentally Ill Can a Psychiatrist/Psychotherapist Be? (Not Too!)

How much psychopathology can a psychiatrist have and still be successful in his or her career? 'Organized psychiatry' and the American Psychiatric Association have gradually edged the concept of "Neurosis" to the periphery and finally out of the diagnostic domain of psychiatry. However, the phenomenology of this diagnosis is alive and well on the human scene and among psychiatrists.. The American Psychiatric Association's (1991) glossary

defines **neurotic process** as:

> "A specific etiological process involving the following sequence:
> *unconscious conflicts* between opposing wishes or between wishes and
> prohibitions lead to unconscious perception of anticipated danger or
> dysphoria, which leads to *defense mechanisms* that result in either symptoms,
> personality disturbance, or both."

I think the reasons for 'modern' psychiatry's tendency to brush Neurosis aside is that

neurotic symptoms involve ever more complex mingling of subtle personality disturbances

and good old neurotic symptoms embedded in character flaws. Long-term psychotherapy is

the treatment of choice for neurosis and neurotic character disorder, but managed care

moguls regard it as too expensive. One of my trusted and clear- thinking mentors once said to

me at supervision, "Give me an 'up-tight', constricted neurotic patient to loosen up any day,

compared to an over-indulged, pampered, entitled, and narcissistically afflicted patient who

takes decades before they learn humility and an effective sense of personal boundaries".

A mild or moderate Neurosis or Neurotic Character disturbance is not a problem for a

psychiatrist. In fact, I think it is rare for a 'normal' personality to choose psychiatry as a

career or be very effective in psychiatry. The Neurosis draws us towards the field, but the

Neurosis must be effectively treated via intensive individual or group therapy, or preferably

both. Individual therapy and analysis can miss some crucial aspects of the future psychiatrists

blind spots that a group therapy experience can be helpful in confronting. These treatments

are essential to reducing our blind spots in working with patients; increasing our empathy for

patients' painful conflicts; and reducing the danger of our acting-out or violating boundaries

with patients. I have become convinced that all psychiatrists need to have an individual

personal psychotherapy and at least two years of group treatment as a part of our training.

This training group and leader need to **specifically** explore with the psychiatrist, his or her

vulnerabilities for acting-out, based on the Family of Origin issues the group has explored with the doctor. These explored areas should include sexual, erotic, financial, aggressive and intimacy anxieties and conflicts. I also believe that psychiatrists in practice should form on-going small groups of trusted colleagues for study, peer supervision, support, vacation coverage and therapeutic work as personal or professional problems arise.

In essence, it is OK or perhaps desirable for us psychiatrists to have a well treated Neurosis or mild character disorder. But, in my opinion, it is unacceptable for a psychiatrist to have Schizophrenia, severe Bipolar disorder, other psychosis, or especially a severe personality disorder such as Borderline, Psychopathic or Addictive types. The danger of acting-out via inappropriate sexual or financial boundary violations with vulnerable patients is too great with these diagnoses. It is a mistake for a psychiatric residency program to accept or graduate a trainee with severe psychopathology, no matter how brilliant or talented they are.

Protection of patients during their treatment is important. We can't allow the danger of exploitation of patients posed by a disturbed and boundary-violating colleagues. The efforts to exclude such psychiatrist exploiters should start early, and never cease. Specific feedback about significant psychopathology in a trainee should be actively sought from his supervisors and peers. This should be structured into the training program, openly discussed and understood up-front before the training experience starts. Annual reviews of a trainee's progress and learning should cover this area effectively. Emotional support and gratitude needs to be extended to those of us who maintain the watch during interviews of would-be psychiatrists and on ethics committees in our psychiatric societies and community. My tragic classmate Jack illustrates my last point poignantly!

The Tragedy of My Residency Classmate Jack

Six weeks before my residency-training group was due to graduate, we were greeted on a Monday morning with the headlines:

"Psychiatrist in training kills himself and his entire family."

Most of our psychiatry department members were away at that time at the national APA Convention. Jack had shot his wife, daughter, and his little five-year -old son--- and then himself. The little boy survived his wounds, but would be incapacitated the rest of his life. After all these years my rage at Jack finally begins to appear. What form of infidelity, insult, deprecation or provocation could warrant such murderous action by my colleague? I still shudder with horror now!

Jack had shared with me once how in his family from a deep southern U S city, he had been A very light skinned African American. He was an only child. His mother and father were very black color. When the family would go to a ball game or county fair, his parents rode in the back of the bus and they insisted that he ride in the front of the bus. He had felt so alone. Jack had not wanted such specialness. He gladly would have rode with his folks at the back of the bus. He hated to get pushed up to the front. I recall joking with Jack that I would have gladly joined him at the back of the bus. He chuckled in appreciation. I recall that his wife and children lived about eighty miles away and he would commute to be with them each weekend when he was not on call at our busy hospital psychiatry service. I met his wife and children at one psychiatry department Christmas party and I recall that his wife and kids were very black in their skin color. Jack had said to me once that he had wished that his wife had acted more comfortable with whites. Had that been a source of conflict again on that ill-fated day?

As soon as it was possible our department chairman held a supportive psychological autopsy session with all of us residents. This group session was helpful, but remnants of the shock, disbelief, pain, and horror are still with me over thirty years later. Our psychological autopsy discussion about Jack reminds me of the old parable about "The Five Blind Men and the Elephant". In our collegial relationships with Jack, we each had isolated pieces of information about how unhappy, insecure, paranoid and disturbed he had been. Like the FBI, CIA and NSC before the 911 terrorist horror events, we each had pieces of information that if shared and correlated, might have averted disaster. Supervisors and particularly Jack's therapist were in my retrospective opinion, unduly concerned about confidentiality and legalities. Major paranoid, psychotic and self-medication behaviors were not reported as the "Buck Never Stopped Anywhere", so effective action could not be taken.

I can recall sharing supervision with Jack and another colleague at a clinic where we had been assigned. The supervisor was trying to help us develop skills of teaching "free-association" to our neurotic outpatients. When Jack's patient finally started to free associate, Jack immediately placed the patient on an antipsychotic medication. Jack had seemed more anxious than his patient and unbeknown to us, had asked his therapist for antipsychotic medication for himself around that same time. Our clinic supervisor seemed concerned about Jack's behavior but treated the incident with humor and a supportive tone.

To this day I do not know how much information the admissions committee had about Jack's problems before he was accepted in our residency, but I know Jack had taken partial training in several other specialties' residency programs. There are obviously no easy answers, but I do think that the stresses of psychiatric training and practice are such that major psychiatric problems in trainees should prohibit admission to or graduation from training programs. All trainees in our profession should know about and sign releases "Up-Front", for thorough discussions of their mental health by teachers, supervisors and colleagues in training. Candid and caring discussions among colleagues in training and faculty need to take place every six months. This process takes courage and should emphasize known negative impact or potential impact on patient care. Perhaps we could create a position as 'psychiatrist researcher' without credentials to work with patients for colleagues who are too vulnerable. It is never too soon to learn that one is not suited for "The Impossible Profession". I know from painful and extensive experience on professional ethics and grievance committees, that it is far more difficult to confront this issue many years on down the road of psychiatric practice. It is vastly more desirable for us to police ourselves through peer confrontation, than for lawyers to do this for us. Safety and best interests of our patients is of ultimate importance.

.

Chapter IV---MONEY AS MOTIVATION For Psychiatrists

Beware of Would-be Psychiatrist Millionaires

The best motivations for a person entering psychiatry are curiosity about and empathy for people. Physician psychiatrists and pediatricians are at the low end of end of the physician pay scale spectrum. However, you will always have a very adequate income as a psychiatrist. If you want millionaire status, go into business or pick your financial advisor carefully. Keeping up with the mushrooming panoply of bio-psycho-social information required in our field precludes us from spending time doing aggressive investing. In fact, the attitude of an aggressive investor may interfere with the quiet empathy and in-depth listening required by our profession.

An Insider Temptation

My patient Doug was in the third year of our work together in his eventually successful five-year psychoanalysis. Doug is a talented physician with a small practice because of the commitment of his time to teaching and research. Doug had worked through some major painful and traumatic losses and had recently remarried after a previous painful divorce. His younger second wife wanted to have several children and wanted to travel. Doug had begun to seek investments to add to his income. His analytic sessions began to focus on these 'money projects' so much that the process had bogged down. He was obsessing at a session about a real estate deal that could bring in a lot of profit with very little risk. I confronted him about what appeared to me to be resistance to the therapy process. Doug grew angry with me saying:

"Olsson, I'm giving you the name of the broker because you can get in on this deal too. A lot of physicians are in on it. Even some of your psychiatrist colleagues."

I told Doug that I could not use information I received in a session as a basis or stimulus to invest. I tried to explore with him the meanings of this 'money project'. What if it failed? He laughed at me and told me that I was too idealistic. The resistance persisted around this topic for several weeks and Doug had equated me with his father who had been a financial failure. The deadline for sign-up for the real estate deal passed and it turned out that Doug had checked frequently to see if my name was on the list of investors. Doug had also heard from a psychiatrist friend of his that the group of psychiatrists I worked with had a solid, successful and conservative investment program that he admired. This allowed Doug to look at a key issue. His father had always promised that Doug's college would be paid for by his father's insurance program. It turned out that the insurance did not mature until long after Doug was out of college. Doug worked part time and got scholarships and loans on his own to get through school. His father used the insurance for his own very modest early retirement. Doug's analysis moved steadily forward after this event. He felt that my honesty and solid ethical stance had been important to him. Doug felt that it allowed him to feel strong and independent, but still involved with me as his analyst.

Chapter V---ABOUT THOSE PSYCHOTHERAPY SKILLS

Can you imagine a physician working in a hospital or clinic without a quality stethoscope and his or her accumulated experience of hearing murmurs, bruits, rubs, bowel sound, etc? Our psychodynamic psychotherapy skills and conduction of a mental status exam are analogous to an experienced cardiologists work with a stethoscope.

Every aspect of psychiatric practice involves some or extensive use of psychodynamic psychotherapy skills. Especially the managed care absurdity called the fifteen minute 'med-check', or the one half hour 'med-eval', require psychotherapy skills. The only way to counter this truth is to use constant denial to gloss-over every emotional cue, transference clue, or hints of relationship problems that your patient presents at an interview.

Psychotherapy Skills Hopefully Embedded in the Practice of Psychopharmacology

As we discuss hoped-for therapeutic effects or possible side effects of medication we intend to prescribe, it is helpful to observe the non-verbal reactions of the patient as well as attending to cognitive questions they pose to us. Many patients give clear messages that they are not ready to take medication after only thirty or forty five minutes of consultation with us. If we charge ahead, hand them a script, and a card with the next appointment time, they will find a way to lose the script, not fill it, or cancel the next appointment. I think this patient also focuses more negatively on side effects that seem more likely to occur. Unless the patient is acutely psychotic or suicidal, it is often helpful to allow the patient to read about the medication and return soon to discuss it further. It is also important to allow discussion of any bad experiences they or their family or friends have had with medications. If they are already in counseling or psychotherapy, it is important to request signed permission to confer with the therapist they have been seeing or the one they will be referred to shortly. If the patient has had several unhelpful therapy experiences; is on multiple medications; has concomitant and complicated medical problems; and or a complicated personality disorder; it is often best for you to do both the psychotherapy and the psychopharmacology. I have great sympathy for psychiatrists who refuse to split the treatment. Rarely is it possible, even if therapist and precriber office in the same building, to have enough time or pay available for collaboration. This collaboration is absolutely necessary in the treatment of Borderline Personality Disorder. The psychotherapist-psychiatrist dyad must try to anticipate splitting, explore projective identifications and crisis creations, which require conjoint sessions and or very frequent phone contact.

In the last decade one of the most difficult tasks for us psychiatrists is to say **NO** about prescribing medication. Our patients have seen TV adds or read on the Internet about antidepressants, mood stabilizers and sleep medications. They all but demand to get a prescription. Very frequently they have already gotten their PCP or internist to prescribe psychiatric medication. After pill-treatment failures, they come to us expecting more specific identification of the "magic pill" for their cure. These situations require careful psychiatric consultation that includes personal and family history of alcoholism and or substance abuse. Such consultations also require careful assessment of vocational, marital, sexual and family communicational issues. I have found that it is important to see this type of patient several times and use my skills to discern transference dynamics toward my office staff or me. If I detect marital, vocational or family communicational issues, I say so. I Recommend that individual, couples or family therapy be tried. Often the patient will fire me on the spot, but I write them a note inviting follow-up discussion several weeks later.

Psychotherapy Skills Useful in Consultation/Liaison Psychiatry

An attractive, articulate and knowledgeable young internist requested that I see her patient on the acute care unit saying over the phone, "My patient won't talk or listen to me. I spent a long time trying to explain things to him."

Ray was a husky, ruddy complected, 75 year old man with a scruffy, salt and pepper beard. As I entered Ray's room his nephew was leaving. I introduced myself to his nephew Sid and asked him if he could wait in the waiting area. I turned to Ray saying:

> "Did Dr. Wayne let you know I would be stopping by? I am Dr. Olsson, a `
> psychiatrist."

Ray spoke loudly,

"I don't need no psychologist!"

Sid had lingered near the door and said with a kind voice tone,

> "Uncle Ray, Dr. Wayne did tell me and Howie that a psychiatrist doctor was coming to see you because you wouldn't talk to her or listen."

Ray complained,

> "That woman can't be a doctor. She looks younger than my know-it-all daughter Julie. She talks down to me when she goes on and on about all them tests and possible surgery. How can I trust her? She bosses me. She scares me."

I sensed the bonding and trust between Sid and Ray.

I asked Ray if he minded if Sid joined us and helped me understand what the doctors were recommending. Sid with a little collaboration with me was able to explain to Ray that he needed a tube passed down into his intestine to relieve the pressure from a blockage. If this didn't work, a surgeon might need to be called to operate. We explained that Dr, Wayne would not be the surgeon and would not see Ray unconscious and naked in the operating room, which Ray secretly feared.

I recommended to Dr. Wayne that she make sure that Howie or Sid was around to help with her explanations to Ray about his medical care. Dr. Wayne was fascinated with importance of these dynamics and grateful for my assistance.

In this case, negative father-daughter transference/countertransference issues clouded the perceptions between Ray and Dr. Wayne. The positive father-son-nephew male bonding was a helpful adjunct in the situation. Supportive psychotherapeutic interventions and psychodynamically founded educational or environmental interventions such as this one are commonly helpful on the hospital medical or surgical units.

Chapter VI---Candidly Assessing Our/Your Training and Experience in Psychotherapy

Be honest with yourself about your training in and experience with psychotherapy. In recent years it is a rare residency program in psychiatry that provides in-depth teaching and supervision in psychotherapy. Most residency programs think they provide adequate psychotherapy training but they do not. This is particularly true when it comes to long term psychodynamic or insight oriented psychotherapy. The core of doing effective psychotherapy beyond a depth of reading is one's own psychotherapy experience.

Questions to Ask When Interviewing a Therapist for Yourself

When you ask these questions, observe the clinician to see if they act defensive, arrogant or annoyed. If they do---go to another therapist for evaluation. It is good for you to interview at least three therapists regardless. It is worth this process because you will be spending a lot of time and money with this person. You do not want them to be controlling or too passive.

(1) Does he or she have a consultant or several consultants for second opinions if it becomes necessary? If the therapist is not a physician, do they have a psychiatrist to consult with if one would be necessary or helpful?

(2) Has the therapist had his own completed psychoanalysis or in-depth psychotherapy? Was the therapist's therapy helpful and successful?

(3) Are there any particular patients they find it difficult to work with?

(4) How many therapy hours per week does the therapist schedule? (I do not think any therapist can effectively treat more than thirty-five hours per week.) If the therapist sees less than ten hours of therapy per week, they may be doing too many other things to be effective. How often does the therapist travel, lecture, or vacation each year? Will this affect the regularity of your sessions? Who would be covering for the therapist if a crisis occurred?

(5) What continuing education and supervision does the therapist make use of?

(6) If your therapy is ever used in case histories or publications what are the therapist's policies and will you see any such material before it is used?

(7) What procedures are established "UP-Front" as to second opinions or consultations should there be any problems or impasse in the treatment?

(8) If there are ethical concerns or questions about the therapists behavior that would be the professional body or organization (with phone number and address) where you could inquire confidentially or in writing?

(9) Does the therapist use any unusual techniques or procedures that would be different than those used by his peers? If so, what are they? How is their use thought to be helpful? Possibly harmful?

(10) What are the therapist's views about your religious or spiritual concerns, if they arise or seem to have importance to you during the treatment?

(11) How will the therapist deal with your spouse, family, children or relatives during the treatment process? Who would he refer your loved ones to if that became necessary or helpful?

(12)   Has the therapist ever had an ethical complaint substantiated against him? Any successful malpractice judgments?

(13)   How old is the therapist and how good is his health?

Chapter VII---BOUNDARY ISSUES AND DANGERS.

Social, Financial and Sexual boundaries are both subtle and consequential in our practice of psychiatry. Over the last fifteen years I have been alarmed and saddened to learn from reliable sources about seven prominent psychiatric or psychoanalytic colleagues who violated professional, sexual and or financial boundaries with their patients or ex-patients. I thought I knew these colleagues and they had had my respect and admiration until I learned about these behaviors. I never cease to be amazed and humbled by the human animal's ability to extend compassion, and our capacity for cruelty, dishonesty and evil. In this chapter I offer my thoughts about these often painful boundary violation issues.

'Routine' Financial and Administrative Boundaries with Patients.

It is best to be clear, up-front, and consistent in administrative policies with patients. Money always needs to be grist-for-the-mill and an effective domain for limit-setting and insight. Insight gained, the meaning of, and behavioral changes around money are only lasting ---AFTER effective work with the patient about his or her responsibility about the boundary involving money is complete. Rarely does a patient get much benefit from treatment if they get away with cheating me out of money they have owed me. Collection of over-due fees has always been better achieved when I did not let the bill build up too much before I dealt clearly with my patient about their bill. If I used a collection agency I always insisted on the process being as dignified and respectful, but as firm and straightforward as possible.

After trying many ways of doing it, I found that a written statement about my policies about scheduling, payment, cancellations, vacations, illness, insurance forms, managed care communications, weekend and evening calls, coverage and emergencies is most effective. There needs to be a place for the patient or their parent to sign and for me to witness. That is the best way to handle these matters. A copy for the patient to take with them and another for my file was imperative. Regardless, confusion still occurs at times. When medications were involved in addition to therapy, I provided written material about the medication and related issues. I gave a summary of the major risks, possible rewards, and major side effects. I invited them to call me if they had major questions about the medication treatment.

With teenagers I told them that I would not reveal anything they told me to their parents or authorities unless someone's life was in danger. If parents pushed for meetings with me I would try to get my teenager to agree, but I always included my teenage patient in the meeting and sometimes recommended therapy for the parent, the parental couple, or the family with another therapist I trusted and would stay in touch with about important issues.

Sexual and Intimacy Boundaries

A high percentage of successful malpractice claims against psychiatrists occurs in the area of 'undue familiarity'. We psychiatrists can also be sued for 'vicarious liability' for the acts of therapists we supervise.* Our concern as professionals must not just be the fear of financial loss from a malpractice judgment. Sexual boundary violations with a patient, former patient or family member of a patient, no matter how they are rationalized by a psychiatrist, are always associated with psychological trauma. They are always to be regarded as unethical. In my experience, they are impossible or extremely difficult for a subsequent therapy to resolve for the ex-patient and the ex-therapist.

Patients to be Wary of, and Who Require Extensive Consultation/Supervision.

Even though we have had excellent training it does not mean that we can treat every patient we evaluate. This is particularly true when we do intensive psychotherapy but is also true for some psychopharmacology cases. Humility, self-awareness and wisdom are never gained soon enough in our profession. Some patients with narcissistic, borderline or hysterical character disorders can be exciting or alluring. This is particularly true if the patient is perceived as sexy, handsome or beautiful by the psychiatrist. Our fantasies can run wild with notions of rescue; 'love-cure' or Pygmalion themes.

Erotic and Erotized Transference/Countertransference.

If you practice psychodynamic psychotherapy that involves two or more sessions per week, you will observe and make use of many intense transference reactions occurring in the interactions with your patient. If you have had a good personal psychotherapy and supervision, you will make good use of your counter transference reactions to help the patient understand him or herself.

Sometimes however, severe character pathology or fragility is missed or cannot be detected even at five or six evaluation sessions. If you have questions or uneasy intuitions during the evaluation of a patient for intensive psychotherapy, it can often be very valuable to get psychological testing. Extremes on the MMPI Baron's ego strength scale or "Borderline"Rorschach responses can be important indicators for recommending less intensive forms of treatment. I have found that this is an excellent time to use referral to a psychologist who both knows the Rorschach test and the domain of psychotherapy practice.

After several evaluation sessions it can be helpful to offer a trial interpretation or two to any patient being considered for psychotherapy. The patient's response is important to observe. If they react with minimal anxiety and a curiosity that leads to deeper reflection, it is a good sign. If the patient shows no collaborative effort at self-understanding and continues self-absorbed symptom descriptions, be wary. Beware of a patient that develops abrupt erotic, aggressive, idealizing or devaluing responses toward you at the first few evaluation sessions. If your intuition whispers cautions in your ear, a consultation with a respected and experienced colleague about suitability for intensive psychotherapy or psychoanalysis is always good psychiatric practice.

Richard Chessick* as early as 1971, talked about what he called the "Neurosis of Abandonment". Chessick uses "Borderline" to refer to the borderline between severe neurosis or neurotic character disorder and psychosis. In other words, these patients do not seek insight and the use of it for their further autonomy and self-actualization. Rather, they use the relationship with us to prevent their suicidal, homicidal or psychotic behaviors. Chessick had the courage to discuss his failures in the treatment of these patients, which can be valuable for our learning to avoid intensive psychotherapy with them. Once in such a quagmire, consultation with a trusted colleague is imperative.

Genuine Falling in Love with a Patient, Ex-patient, Student, or Supervisee.

Unfortunately these situations are not extremely rare. It is very rare however, for these relationships to result in a happy or contented long-term relationship. This is because of the ubiquitous, powerful and unresolved transference and counter transference issues as well as the imbalance of social power and control. This is even true if a successful therapy was completed with the patient. It is probably due to the imbalance in power between the physician psychiatrist and the patient/student/supervisee. A successful therapy of the psychiatrist may in some cases prevent the romance with a patient from occurring, but once the love affair is in full bloom, psychotherapy can never get the genie back in the bottle. I know of only two successful marriages of psychiatrists and former patients, but in both instances the wife-former patients were independently wealthy and the relationships led to many painful social and professional struggles and dilemmas.

I once treated the third wife of a psychiatrist. The psychiatrist had divorced his first wife to marry a patient. He then left his second wife to marry yet another patient. His third wife sought my help when her husband the psychiatrist was found to be having yet another love affair with a current patient. In each marriage the "Me Psychological Tarzan, you patient Jane" dimension, only emerged when the day-in, day-out domain of married life arrived. The exciting romance was great. The aftermath and home-life was not. The masochistic and self-defeating character disorder traits were florid in this psychiatrist. His brilliance in the cognitive domain did not help him at all.

Often these situations lead to complicated ethical and legal proceedings. I (Olsson****, 1994) have advocated that a psychiatrist ombudsperson be appointed to serve as a support for the violated patient, student or supervisee. This psychiatrist as well as a probono lawyer if the person can't afford an attorney, allows for neutralization of the massive power differential that so often skews this process in favor of the offending psychiatrist. Rarely does the reverberating mirror of idealization between psychiatrist and patient lead to "Happy-ever-afters", if they challenge the Gods and marry. Neurosis and the Oedipal Complex are alive and well in these situations.

The Ultimately Poignant Boundary: Our Role and Responsibilities When a Patient Commits Suicide.

In my 35 years of psychiatric practice I can recall two patients who were in active treatment with me when they chose to commit suicide. I had several other patients who I learned later had committed suicide at various time periods after they ended treatment with me. During the six years I worked as a psychiatrist on a community mental health center's team for the treatment of severely and chronically mentally ill patients, we had several patients who committed suicide. In the aftermath of our patient's suicides; our attending their funerals; our work with the grieving families; our own grief-work as a mental health team was moving and important for everyone.

In the two suicides of the patients in my private practice, I was unable to attend either of these talented young men's funerals, which were held in distant locations. However, I had lengthy phone conversations with both of their mothers. These contacts were very important for the patients' mothers and for me. In both cases what seemed very important for these grieving mothers was to be reassured in an authentic way that they or their husbands were not the 'cause' of their son's suicide. In both instances there had been difficult relationships with their fathers, but that had not been the cause of their suicides. I was impressed with the importance of the candor of our discussions about the difficult father-son relationships, but also the detailed discussion of how complex the causality of their suicides were. In one instance, it became very important for the mother to pay me for one of two final sessions her son had scheduled with me, but not the last session, which was scheduled for after the day of her son's suicide. The mother's comment was, "Dr. Olsson, I wish my son had kept that appointment with you, because I can tell you were really trying to help him. Fred told me that the last time we talked over the phone." I had had no indication that her son was contemplating suicide beyond a dawning awareness about how delusional he was. I was shocked when I learned that her son, my patient, had been found hanging from a windmill out on a deserted stretch of rural highway. During the several months I knew Fred, I had finally begun to learn about the depth of his schizoid personality structure and self-loathing that involved religious delusional perceptions. I had begun to wonder if he was not taking the antipsychotic medication that I had prescribed. Fred had assured me that he was taking the medication. After I listened at length to Fred's mother, I assured her during our phone conversation that she and her husband were not the cause of their son's suicide.

After both of these suicides, I found comfort and support from my weekly peer

supervision and a journal article / book discussion group of trusted colleagues. In one of the

cases, I also got help from a clergyperson who listened in detail about some of the

complicated religious and ethical issues with which the other of my deceased patients had

been struggling.

John was a talented 40-year-old divorced surgeon in a busy subspecialty practice. I had been his supervisor on his inpatient rotation during his medical school rotation in psychiatry. He sought me out for psychotherapy when his marriage broke up and he found himself in turmoil when he "Came-out" into a gay lifestyle. After six months in therapy, he had become less frenetic and impulsive in his homosexual relationships. However, he developed mild symptoms of ARC, and turned HIV positive. Though John of course was anxious, he was only mildly depressed. There were no psychotic disturbances of thought. He trusted me with his careful plan to commit suicide. He had been a very dedicated physician, and had in fact operated upon the local rich and famous. This included some of the most famous physicians in the city. John anticipated the lawsuits, the anxiety, and the devaluing rumors that would arise around his name and reputation. At age 40, he preferred to carefully commit suicide in the rural area of his birth, rather than drag hundreds of his patients and colleagues through the anxiety and fear that would occur if "The Public" knew of his AIDS. I tried to explore the neurotic aspects of this preoccupation. I all but threatened to commit John to a local facility or the state hospital. I consulted with two trusted colleagues who both urged me to ' listen to my patient, and not the textbook'. I offered more frequent appointments and hospitalization to John who expressed disappointment in me because I did not grasp his perspective or 'ultimate concerns'. At the final session with John, I knew at a conative level that he would commit suicide that weekend, and that I would never see him again. When I expressed that intuition to John, he smiled, hugged me, and calmly left my office. The next week I got the call from his mother about the death of her beloved and worshipped son. She somehow knew that it was a suicide, though the local coroner, who was John's childhood mentor, said it was 'natural'. I helped John's mother to understand the complicated circumstances that John faced before his death decision. I was very candid but very empathic with her. I expressed my doubts and fears about my 'clinical judgment and decision-making' with the priest I trusted. The prayer offered by me and the priest at the end of my time with this clergyperson was very important to me. It has helped me to never look back in doubt, guilt or shame.

I have found one excellent journal article and one important books that I highly

recommend.

Neil S. Kaye MD, and Stephen M. Soreff MD have written a cogent, clear,

comprehensive, and helpful article entitled, "The Psychiatrist's Role, Responses, and

Responsibilities When a Patient Commits Suicide". It is located in the American Journal of Psychiatry, June 1991, Vol148: 6, pp739-743.

Finally, I want to mention Doctor Sue Chance's powerfully important book, STRONGER THAN DEATH: When Suicide Touches Your Life. (1992), W.W. Norton & Company. Dr. Chance shares the poignant array of feelings she experienced after the suicide of her son. The courage, candor/catharsis, and compassion expressed through her book is of such value that it can be of benefit to your work and can be recommended for patients and their families to read. Dr, Chance is a gifted writer. She courageously tackles the issue of anger at the deceased in the surviving loved ones of the suicide. Her love never wavered toward her dead son but she is honest about how strong her anger was as well.

Chapter VIII---RETIREMENT: A FORBIDDEN TOPIC, TREASURED GOAL, OR SHIBBOLETH?

Don't wait too many years before thinking carefully about the R word.

Psychiatry and psychotherapy can provide a vocational lifetime of intellectual, emotional and ethical challenges. The human domains of brain, body, mind and spirit provide a psychiatrist with an infinite number of opportunities for experiences of curiosity, wonder, frustration, sadness and humility. I have always considered psychiatry and psychotherapy to be a calling, and not just a profession. Our bio-psycho-social ideal of approach to human problems involves an art and a science. It is difficult not to get swept up in narrow "Scientism/reductionism" of neuropsychiatry, or a wild subjectivity of intuitive psychotherapy interpretations that have no basis in solid observation based upon careful listening to patients over adequate periods of time.

Some psychiatrists find their center of creativity and vocational challenge in their work. They are fully content to spend fifty years or more in clinical work. They are content to "die-in-the-saddle" or retire when their health begins to fail. An admired child psychiatrist friend and colleague of mine in his seventies said to me recently, "I love my work each day." He is a gifted helper for his child and adult patients.

Other colleagues are conscientious and dedicated to their work, but are just as eager to go home after work and study finances, paint, sculpt, study music, garden or write poetry. There are many career trajectories possible in psychiatry. Sometimes burnout occurs and the only resolution of it is a career-shift or change. To fight-off or ignore the intuition that a career change is best can sometimes lead to stagnation, boredom and even boundary violations with patients. I know of one colleague who spent increasing time talking about business and moneymaking deals during his workday, even with some of his patients.

Some colleagues have especially sensitive souls. Years of hearing about the pain, suffering, grief, loss, trauma and despair of patients begins to drain them beyond available treatments for burnout. They are not weak, neurotic or depressed. One admired colleague who had been an excellent child psychotherapist for twenty-five years is now enjoying being a teacher and composer of music. He said to me, "I guess I drew an overly loaded case load of wounded, traumatized kids that required so much of me to treat". Some of his music I think reflects transcendence of pain and trauma in the soaring sounds and lyrics he has created.

Psychiatry offers a range of potential career shifts within the field. Teaching, research, and administration are such areas of opportunity. Our psychiatry and psychotherapy skills can be applied to business and applications in undergraduate or graduate school teaching. One semester I co-taught for six hours each week with a friend who is a professor of English. I used psychodrama and pedagogic drama techniques to enliven the student's study of Faulkner and Tennessee Williams.

"Retirement Myths" are common and often are dysfunctional fantasies of only idle time for only relaxed fishing, golf, tennis and travel. At its best, retirement means claiming time for doing more of what you enjoy and find meaningful or challenging. It at its best requires a balance of activities and certainly keeping a lively mind, spirit and community involvement. Don't fear or idealize retirement, plan for it and enjoy it.

Chapter IX---PARTING THOUGHTS.

Thank you for attending to my pontifications and advice; especially my cathartic journeys based upon residual, unresolved pain from my efforts to practice psychiatry and psychotherapy with as much integrity and ethical fabric as I knew how. I hope judgments I have made about clinical practice and personal life was for the most part not judgmental.

Sincerely,

Peter A. Olsson M.D.